Linux is Badass

Other works by Bryan Lunduke

Linux for Hank
Road-Sign Hank & the Aliens
2299 : Act One

Linux is Badass
by Bryan Lunduke

2nd Edition, published 2018

Linux is Badass.
(Slightly More Badass Edition)

by Bryan Lunduke

ISBN 978-1-365-05209-5

Ordering Information can be found at:
www.Lunduke.com

Table of Contents

A Very Boring Introduction

Over the years I've written a boatload of articles about Linux. Not a big boat, mind you. Possibly only a medium sized boat, but a boat nonetheless, and it was somewhat loaded. Most of those articles being firmly in the "safe for work" camp. Reviews, editorials, breaking news – fine, upstanding journalist-y stuff.

But, on occasion, I just don't feel like being upstanding.

That is where this book comes in. This book is foul-mouthed and ridiculous. This is my outlet for being profane and stupid – with a few intelligent thoughts (purely accidental, I swear) hidden underneath the F-bombs and neck-beard jokes.

This book is like that little valve on a hot water heater that releases steam, whenever the pressure gets too great, so that the damned thing doesn't turn into a missile. Except, instead of steam, it's boner jokes. Ergo, this book is the only thing that kept me from turning into a boner joke missile. Which is now a real thing. Because I just wrote those words together.

After I pulled together a few pieces, I realized it worked as a book. Maybe not a classy book. Nor a long book. But a book. Definitely, technically a book. But there was something missing... something that I didn't realize right away.

What this book needed... was a choose your own adventure story.

Why not, right? I'd already written a chapter called "It just works? Fuck that!" so why limit myself? I loved choose your own adventure books as a kid and figured an adventure focused on Linux would fit right in with the rest of this absurd collection of words.

So I wrote that and slapped it right on the end. Because

that's just the kind of book this is.

[Pro Tip: In various parts, throughout the book, you will find some some portions in square brackets. Just like this paragraph. Those are little asides I added in after I finished the book, and went back over it and had thoughts that I wanted to add to whatever it is I had written. You can safely skip over the bracketed portions and still get the gist of things. Usually.]

A Badass Introduction.

What you are about to read is one seriously fucking important book. Every single, g-d damn word.

Because Linux is badass. Seriously badass. We're talking Sylvester Stalone and Chuck Norris had their genes combined to create a clone baby. And that baby kicked a football to the moon. And then the moon fucking exploded. And fucking candy flew out. Good candy too, not like fucking red vines or some shit like that.

["not like fucking red vines or some shit like that". Hemingway, eat your heart out.]

This is a book about that. About Linux. And Linux achieving such stellar levels of badassery.

Don't know what Linux is? Fuck you. This book isn't for you. Stop reading right now and go buy a book about the history of tampons; you can't handle this book. How the shit did you even manage to find this book?

[Yay! Alienating my potential customer base! I'm going to make millions!]

Know what Linux is but don't think it's baddass? Read this book. Read the shit out of this book. When you're done you'll know why you were being such a complete dumb-ass.

[Huh. So, in my head, apparently "badass" is just one, plain old normal word and "dumb-ass" is hyphenated. I almost deleted these last few lines during editing for fear that they would offend folks. But I decided to keep them. Because that's more badass.]

9

In order to declare something to be officially fucking badass, we must first create a baseline from which we can measure. So let's take a look at all the other piece of shit operating systems out there to see if any of them are badass or not.

Let's start with an exercise. Stand up, wherever you are, and say the following:

"OH SNAP! Did you see that copy of Windows that he's running on that PC over there? That's just like the one my Aunt Tabitha uses! Badass! I am blown away by how homogeneously hardcore that is!"

Now take note of the fact that you feel like a retard just for saying that. In fact, this is the first time, in human history, that those words have been put together in that order. And it caused three of my fingers to spontaneously erupt into flames while I typed them out.

[They didn't, actually. I'm just pulling your leg there. My fingers are fine.]

"But, what about a Mac? Those are pretty cool!" I hear some of you saying.

No. No they are not. And you are a bad person for having said so. Here. Let me help you out with a flowchart.

...

Ah, fuck it. I'm too lazy to make a flowchart. Just imagine one where there's a fuck-ton of arrows leading from

"You Think Using a Mac is Cool" to "You Are a Bad Person".

But why? Why are those other systems such steaming piles of donkey crap when compared with the badass – and minty fresh – awesomeness of Linux? Excellent question!

One might think that Linux is great simply by its very nature of not being Windows or MacOS. But that thought would be wrong. Let me paint a kick-ass picture for you.

During a major league baseball game, you come up to bat.

I know. Sports metaphor. Stick with me here.

You step up to the plate, grip your bat, do that thing all baseball players do where they kick the dirt a little bit, and gaze out at the opposing team's pitcher. Right about then you notice that he doesn't seem to be getting ready to throw the ball at you at all. In fact he looks like he's taking a wicked shit in his pants. Then he sits down, right there on the pitcher's mound, and eats a ham sandwich.

[Seriously. What the fuck is the deal with that thing where they kick the dirt as they step up to the home plate? Was the dirt not level enough? Was there something sparkly down there and they just needed to check it out real quick? Makes no damned sense.]

Looking around you notice all the other players on the field are also sitting down, pants full of their own doody, eating ham sandwiches.

This does not mean that you are the best fucking baseball player to ever play the game. All it means is that you didn't shit yourself and eat a ham sandwich. At least, not right at that moment.

[Though, now that I think about it, that is a good first step!]

It means is that you have a chance. The other players' incontinence (and non-Kosher diets) have given you an opportunity – a shot at being badass. What you do with that shot is up to you.

Now... I'm not saying that Windows and MacOS have full britches (in the not-awesome way). But they are about as far from badass as you can get. And that not only gave Linux the opportunity to badass it up, but the motivation as well.

"Motivation? How does having Windows and MacOS metaphorically crap themselves give motivation to... anyone?"

Nature abhors a vacuum.

"Whut?"

If a field has no plants, some will soon grow. If you have a tribe of warriors, one man must rise up to lead them. If no badass Operating System exists, one must be made.

And that, my dear friends, is why Linux is badass. Because it must be.

"It just works"? Fuck that!

Let me tell you a little story.

Once upon a time, there was a perfectly average little boy. Let's call him Stanley.

From the time Stanley was born, until his 18th birthday, he never had to work a single day. No after school jobs, no mowing lawns for neighbors. What about chores around the house? Surely he must have helped clean his room at least! Nope. Never did that either. In fact, Stanley had never even washed a spoon. His spoons were automatically cleaned. By spoon cleaning fairies or some shit like that.

Whenever young Stanley was on the verge of getting hungry, food would magically appear before him. And, not just any ordinary food... awesome food. The exact food that he had been craving, without him even knowing that he was craving it.

Stanley had never experienced the concept of "inconvenience". The cable guy always showed up on time -- without making him wait around all day. Never did Stanley have to wait on hold on the phone. Never accidentally stepped in a puddle, causing his shoe to fill with nasty, street water.

Stanley was the most boring little fucker on the planet.

Was it his fault that he never had any of those life experiences that give the rest of us our character? No. No it wasn't. It was probably the fault of some asshole sorcerer who cast a spell on him... or something. But, you know what? It doesn't matter. He's still a boring little fucker that none of us want to hang out with. (Unless our spoons are dirty and we feel lazy.)

Let's look at the flip side of that example. Let's look at Edward, the guy that lives right next door to boring-as-fuck

Stanley.

On Edward's first day of kindergarten, he accidentally walked down to the mud factory (which, in case you were wondering, is a factory... that makes mud) and applied for, and got, a job. That's right, young Edward, quite unintentionally, was now a full time mud-maker. 7 am to 5pm every day.

And when Edward got home, he had to clean his room. Because his baby sister had been in there. Again. The effect was not unlike a crazed, little tornado.

Oh, and food! Poor, poor Edward. When he wanted a burger, he got a pizza. When he wanted a pizza, he got a burger. When he was interested in neither a pizza nor a burger... he got both (with one inside the other).

Edward is, unlike Stanley, not at all boring. In fact, Edward is a generally awesome dude that is fun to hang out with. He knows what it's like to work hard, which means he is also quite familiar with playing hard as well. And the stories! Edward's stories, though predominantly about working in a mud factory, are the hit of every party.

There is a simple lesson we can learn from this:

Mac users are boring as fuck and shouldn't be invited to parties. Ever.

[Man. I just know some Mac fanboy is going to throw this back at me as proof that I think Macintoshes are great somehow.]

If everyone on earth drives a 1993 Toyota Corolla... nobody has a badass car.

My first car was a 1989 Buick LeSabre. All white on the outside and all red on the inside. It was a boat of a car. Huge. Difficult to park. And it sucked down gas like an [offensive, racist metaphor to use for someone who drinks something really fast].

But I loved it. The ride was smooth and the red-leather bench seats made this the ultimate car to take to a drive-in movie. Driving it made me feel like a pimp. Which was a pretty amazing accomplishment for this pasty, skinny little nerd. And, even more importantly, I could afford it on my meager earnings as a dish-washer-turned-printer-repair-man.

The car was unique (or about as unique as most mass produced cars get). It had style. It had personality.

... It got totaled by a truck delivering cheese only a few short years after I drove it off the lot.

[Seriously. A cheese truck plowed into that poor Buick. Stupid cheese truck.]

One of my co-workers, at the time, had a 1993 Toyota Corolla. In blue. A perfectly fine car. Drove well and got reasonably good mileage – certainly it guzzled the gas at a far more reasonable pace than my big old Pimp-mobile.

There was just one, glaring, problem with that '93 Corolla: It seemed like every single other person in the greater Seattle metropolitan area had one too. Also in blue.

At first, he thought that was awesome. Driving around town he would smile and waive if he pulled up next to another person in this particular car owner club. Lots and lots of waving. And smiling.

15

As the months dragged on, the smile vanished, with the wave turning into more of a limp raising of the pointer finger – without actually removing the hand from the steering wheel – in order to let the other Corolla-ite know that he had, indeed, noticed that they were driving the same damned car.

Eventually even that little finger-raising thing went away too. Replaced, instead, by him adamantly refusing to make eye-contact with anyone driving that accursed car. I call this "Adam's Grumpy Corolla Period".

Oh, yeah, the guy's name was Adam. I forgot to mention that. Well. Truth be told his name is pretty irrelevant. We could change it to "Steve" and the story would be the same. You know what? Forget that I even told you his name. It'll be more mysterious and exciting that way.

The "Grumpy Period", for this UNNAMED DUDE OF MYSTERY, continued for quite a long time. Maybe a year or so. Not joking. This man really started to hate his efficient little blue car. Not through any fault of the cars, mind you – the car was just doing its job. And it did it well enough. Got him from point A to point B. Never broke down. It wasn't the roomiest or most comfortable car around, but it certainly did what it was designed to do.

He resented it. Even started kicking the tires.

And not in that "I'm going to tap the tires with my feet in order to see if they're of good quality" way. More in the "Take that you piece of shit car" way. It was hard to watch this Man-Car relationship, that started out with so much love and hope... devolve into something so... sucky.

[Seriously. What's the deal with "kicking the tires"? Why do people do that? Are there really cars out there that falls apart when a person kicks a tire lightly? Does the wheel just pop off?]

But, eventually, all his negative car-feelings lost steam. His spirit was broken by the blue, metal (and plastic) beast.

16

About this point he began to reconnect with the rest of the Corolla-driving world. Not in an angry way, nor in a happy way. What was once a smile and waive had become... a shrug. Here, let me walk you through a typical experience:

Adam... I mean SOME GUY... pulls up to a stop light in his little blue car. Right next to his car is another one, just like his – only in a slightly different shade of blue – driven by another man who also looks like he's had his will broken.

The two men make eye contact.

One man shrugs and cocks his head, ever so slightly, to the side. As if to indicate "Yeah. I know. Piece of shit car, right?".

The other man does that thing that's half-way between a smile and a frown and slowly, and slightly, nods his head. Closing his eyes for just an instant, as if weeping, quietly, deep down. They understand each others pain.

At that moment any car could pull up beside them... and that third car would instantly be awesome. Just by it's very nature of being different. A beat up pick-up truck with a duct taped muffler and mudflaps with busty ladies on it. One of those tiny little two-seaters that look like plastic escape pods. Or my big, old boat of an '89 Buick. All would be made instantly more awesome by simply not being the same as every other damned car.

Now, I'm not big on the whole "using cars as a metaphor for computers" thing. Been overdone. And, really, it doesn't even apply most of the time. Computers and cars are, as you may have noticed, not the same thing. But, in this particular case, I'm going to force this analogy to work. (And, yes, I know that a "metaphor" is not the same thing as an "analogy"... but I'm going to force that to be the case as well. Through sheer will power.)

Let's do an experiment. Go around and look at the faces of people using PC's running Windows. Doesn't matter what they're doing. Note the look of distant sadness in their eyes.

Then sit down next to them with your laptop, running Linux. You could be using any flavor of Linux. Any Desktop Environment -- KDE, GNOME, Unity... it truly doesn't matter. Don't say a word. Don't make a point of showing them what your computer screen looks like or what you are running... just make sure they can see it out of the corner of their eye.

[Yes. There are multiple people... but they only have one eye, between them, of which they can see out of the corner of.]

Give it a few minutes. Wait until they've definitely noticed that you're not running Windows.

What you do from there is entirely up to you. Just note two things:

1. You have just made another human being, who had already had his will broken by a boring Operating System, even more sad.

2. You are awesome.

Say GNU/Linux One More Time. I dare ya.

I get in a fair bit of trouble for not saying "Gee-En-You-Forward-Slash-Linux". As most of you probably know, that is what Richard Stallman, and a bunch of other guys, like to call any Linux distro.

The reason they like to call it "GNU/Linux" instead of just plain old "Linux" is that many of the GNU projects (such as the GCC compiler) are pretty critical to building and using a system sitting on top of the Linux kernel. That logic makes total sense. So I get where they're coming from.

Unfortunately I simply cannot call it "GNU/Linux". You know why? Because it is a stupid, fucking name. It just is. It sounds dumb. It looks dumb. And it makes me feel like a dumb-ass whenever I say it.

Shit. We could call the entire system "puppy fart infection" for all I care. I would still use it and love it.

In fact, I think it's damned weird that anyone would care about what people call Linux. As long as we all use the same words (or close) so that we know what we're all talking about, that's good enough for me.

No. I'm wrong on that. It's not weird that someone would care. Because, obviously, I care. Otherwise I wouldn't be writing this little ditty right now. What's weird is that someone would make a big stink about it. Such as Richard Stallman refusing to speak at events that use the word "Linux" without also putting a "GNU/" in front of it.

[Wait. Shit. I say it's weird that someone would make a stink about it... when I am making a stink about it. Fuck. I'm loosing this argument with myself.]

I mean, if you're going to make a stink about a name that

refers to a big group of software, built by a large number of people, at least make the name a good one. RoboSharkLazer or something. That way it's more fun for me.

That's really a key point, I suppose. I'd really appreciate if everyone chose project names that I found amusing.

Another thing that irks me: being adamant about calling it "GNU/Linux" is making a point that multiple projects and people contributed significantly to whatever Linux distro you are running. Now, I'm all for people and projects getting proper credit. But if we're going to feel compelled to name our Operating System by creating a large list of included project names (with lots of forward slashes) things would get fucking ridiculous in a heartbeat.

GNU/Linux/Qt/GTK/ncurses/wget/Firefox/GNOME/KDE /GEdit... on and on it goes. Until someone punches me in the nose. To cut all of those projects out of that name would be extremely disrespectful to them.

And, really, even then that doesn't feel properly indicative of the actually system being used. Why is "GNU" listed first? Wouldn't it make more sense to list the project names in order of closeness to the hardware? The GNU tools really sit on top of the Linux kernel (in a way). So "Linux/GNU" would make far more sense.

All of which tells me that the whole "GNU/" thing is pure vanity. Which... I am totally, completely okay with. I love vanity. I am one vain mother-fucker. [This is true.] But I also like it when people, in the act of being vain, simply own up to it. Owning up to vanity is badass.

Badass Leadership.
(Or "My crazy, neck beard dude can beat up your marketing dude.")

Steve Balmer, the current CEO of Microsoft, has a reputation of being... a bit intense. He has a tendency to get up in front of the Microsoft faithful and, while taking on the role of the cheerleader, work himself into a minor frenzy. "Developers, Developers, Developers, Developers" goes the chant.

His enthusiasm for what he does, and what people within his company do, is tangible. And, let's be honest, that can be rather charming. In a sweaty, frightening way.

[Overly long side note: Back during the release of Windows 2000, I worked at Microsoft. Specifically I worked on a team building Windows Media Player for Mac OS and Solaris – which was a totally real thing. Despite me having no real involvement in the Windows 2000 launch itself, I got to go to the launch party. Which had laser tag. Which was pretty fucking sweet. Wait. Why did I bring this up? Oh, right. Balmer. So Balmer was there to speak to the crew. I ended up standing in the front row, with my plate of party food, when he took the stage. Many things were said to get the troops excited. But then something... intense happened. He jumped into talking about Linux. Specifically how much he hates it. "I. HATE. LINUX." He really got into it. When all was said and done there was a significant number of spittle drops on my glasses and I scooted out of there in a hurry. I don't say this to suggest that Balmer spit on me (though, technically, he did)... but to show just how damned passionate and animated the man is.]

Balmer has style (or, at least, a style). Balmer has personality. He may not be your cup of tea, but you can't deny those two facts. Just the same, at the end of the day, Balmer is a salesman. He's in marketing. Which severely limits his awesome potential.

Let's look at the flip-side of that coin: Richard Stallman.

Stallman, the founder of the Free Software Foundation and the GNU project, is... Oh, jeeze. How do I say this... He is a strange little dude with a big beard.

Stallman makes over-the-top statements about an almost mind-boggling number of topics. Wondering what he thinks about human beings having sex with dolphins? Well, my friend, that is damned convenient. Because he's talked about it and you can find his ideas on Man-Dolphin love (which you can never, ever get out of your head again) right on the Internet.

Want to watch a video of him picking shit off his feet, and eat it (and go back for seconds), while he addresses an entire room full of Linux users? Bam. On the Internet. (Again... no chance you can forget that. Some things simply cannot be unseen.)

Now I'm not saying this to demonstrate anything bad about Stallman. Quite the contrary. These examples (which are 2 of roughly 5 million bat-shit-crazy things that the man has said or done over the years) simply prove two simple points.

1. Richard Stallman doesn't give a flying fuck what you think of him. He's going to do shit his way.
2. Richard Stallman "thinks outside the box".

When I say "thinks outside the box", I don't mean it in that uber-annoying corporate way – like when you're manager, at your performance review, instructs you to spend more time "thinking outside the box" and you just kinda want to punch him in the eye-ball.

No. I'm talking about REALLY thinking outside the box.

Here. Let me illustrate with an example.

Normal "Thinking Outside The Box" : You need to ship a box of CD's to Florida by tomorrow morning -- but it's too late to use conventional shipping services. So you buy a plane ticket and fly over to Florida that night to get the CD's there on time.

REALLY "Thinking Outside The Box" : Same problem. More awesome solution. Create a black hole that eats the entire land-mass between you and Florida -- thus making Florida suddenly within walking distance, even from Australia (which is 18 million miles away from anything). Sure, millions of people were killed in the process. But at least you didn't need to fly on the red-eye.

That right there is the big difference between your average, every day technology company leaders and the kind of leaders we have in the Open Source and Linux world. Where most projects are led by reasonable people with, potentially, a few quirks -- we, in the Linux world, get crazy mother-fuckers who will eat those reasonable peoples' brains, absorb their power, then attack Los Angeles with an army of radioactive rodents.

And Stallman is but one example. The Linux world is lousy with folks with similar inclinations and endless power.

Also neck beards. A lot of our guys have neck beards.

Linux is Badass – The Adventure

What follows is an old school, choose your own adventure style... adventure. At the top right corner of each page you will find a number indicating which part of the story you are on, such as "Part 1". Then, as you read, you will be presented with choices of what to do next – and corresponding parts that you should turn to.

It's a pretty simple mechanic. If you don't get it, just pretend like you do. Or people will make fun of you on the Internet.

And by "people", I mean me. And your mom.

[Wooo! Worked in a "mom" joke!]

I should also note that there is, most definitely, a "right path" to follow in this adventure. And I think you'll be smart enough to quickly figure out what that right path is. In fact, if you follow the right path the entire adventure is pretty quick, easy and pleasant. If you deviate from that path though, shit can get bad in a hurry.

And, with that, we begin...

Part 1

OPERATING SYSTEM NOT FOUND

That's all. Just a black screen and those words, in pale white, on your gorgeous new 32" LCD screen. At least you know your newly built computer is working. The RAM check passed and, apparently, you managed to shove the CPU into the right spot. That wasn't a foregone conclusion, so you're pretty psyched about that little victory.

You fold your arms across your chest and lean back, confidently, in your chair – smiling and slowly nod your head. You probably look badass right now. Like a young Charlton Heston after showing those damned dirty apes a what-for.

The smile vanishes as the meaning of those bold, all-caps words slowly dawns on you: You had forgotten to get an Operating System to put on your new, glorious tower of a computer. Luckily, there's only a few real choices, right?

1) Choose Windows - turn to part 4

2) Choose MacOS - turn to part 5

3) Choose Linux - turn to part 6

4) Choose DOS - turn to part 2

As luck would have it, you happen to have a few DOS floppies laying in a box right by your desk.

Why these floppies are in the box, and why the box is, itself, right next to your desk, would make for an interesting story. One involving old boxes filled with old computer crap. Pretty riveting stuff.

Also lucky: the fact that you had the foresight to install a floppy drive in your brand new PC. Sure, floppies are outdated. But what if you "needed do get some important files off a floppy sometime" you thought to yourself. The guy down at your local Nerd Stuff, who helped you ring up the parts, made fun of you. Something about him never having seen one in person before. Who's laughing now, kid?

You slide the floppy into the disk drive and reboot.

A:\> SETUP.EXE

The letters are on the screen before you even knew what was happening. It's almost like... your fingers remember. They knew what you needed to type. "It's good to be home", you think to yourself -- confident in your decision to just use DOS.

"What do I need a newer Operating System for anyway? DOS has everything I'd ever need, right?" you say, rather loudly, to the empty room that was busy not giving a shit.

The Setup program finishes up, you reboot and your computer comes to rest at a C:\>... when it dawns on you. You don't actually have any DOS software to run. Also you have no idea how to get online with DOS. The last time you did that was with an old 28.8 modem -- and you don't have one of those.

1) Give up and install Windows - turn to part 4

2) Give up and install MacOS - turn to part 5

3) Regain your sanity and install Linux - turn to part 6

4) Stick to the plan and make DOS work - turn to part 3

They didn't have any of those, newfangled graphical operating systems in the old days! DOS will do just fine!

Oh-ho! What's this? Out of the corner of your eye you spy a Commander Keen install floppy in the box. Looks like this is your lucky day! You slip the floppy in the disk drive, run the installer, and spend the rest of the afternoon enjoying the best that early 1990's gaming could offer.

Around 6pm you realize that you would, in fact, like to have a modern web browser.

1) Give up and install Windows - turn to part 4

2) Give up and install MacOS - turn to part 5

3) Regain your sanity and install Linux - turn to part 6

Just then, you are struck by a brilliant thought. "Everyone uses Windows. I'll just install that."

Unfortunately the most recent copy of Windows you have in your "box of old computer crap" is 3.1. And, as nostalgic as it might be to relive the early 1990's... you just can't bring yourself to install it. So, to the store it is!

After perusing the aisles of your local computer store -- and dodging no less than 37 blue-shirted marauders, assaulting you with a declaration of "Welcome to Nerd Stuff" -- you decide on just picking up a copy of Windows 8. The reason why you decide to buy Windows 8 may remain shrouded in mystery until the end of time... though it may have something to do with the fact tat you wanted to use Windows... and that was the only version available.

1) Head home and install Windows - turn to part 7

2) Get some froyo - turn to part 8

You head straight to the Apple Store to pick up a copy of Mac OS, confident in your, obviously amazing, decision.

"I'd like a copy of your finest MacOS," you declare, to the first Apple Store employee you find, with a ridiculous swagger that you instantly regret.

"MacOS is free," says the Apple dude. "You already have it with your Mac. And updates are free now."

"But, can I buy a copy to do a fresh install?"

Turns out you can. So you do.

1) Time to head home and install this bad mamajama. - turn to part 11

After thinking it over, you decide to put Linux on your new behemoth. Really, you wondered why you even needed to think it over. Kind of an obvious choice really. You want a fast, cool looking system. Boom. Linux. Decision made.

Only one problem. You don't actually have any way to install Linux. And, with no working PC to download Linux, the options are pretty limited. Ah, but where there's a will there's a way. You hop in the car and head down to the college.

The college, you say? Yes. The college. You see, there's two things that you can find at every college on the planet – college girls and Linux CDs.

You head to the computer science department, walk into one of the labs, and begin to say "Hey, anyone have any Linux distribution discs I can use?" but only get as far as "Hey, anyone ha" when someone shoves a DVD into your hand with a penguin drawn onto the top with a purple highlighter.

Just then a college girl strolls by. Not just any college girl... a NERDY college girl. Nay. College WOMAN. You begin to, mindlessly, move towards what, you are pretty sure, is the most amazing lady you've ever seen. She would love to go to Comic Con with you, all you need to do is ask. Of this you are sure.

The man who gave you the Linux DVD speaks, "No, dude. Not yet. You're not ready."

You have no idea what he means by that. But he sounds like a mixture between Yoda and Ted "Theodore" Logan, so you go with it.

1) Celebrate with some froyo - turn to part 14

2) Head home and install Linux - turn to part 15

3) Throw the DVD in his face and install Windows - turn

to part 4

4) Give up your dreams and buy a turtleneck - turn to part
5

5) Break the DVD, go home and install DOS - turn to part
2

You get home, let Scruffy out to go potty, and set about installing Windows 8 on your beast of a PC.

[It should be noted, at this point, that you, the reader, has no idea what "Scruffy" is. Nothing in the sentence above tells you what "Scruffy" is. You assume it is a dog, because it's name is "Scruffy". You know what that is? That's racist. You are racist. What if it's a cat? Or a person with real person feelings. You also assume that "Scruffy" is a boy. Which also makes you sexist. You are a sexist, racist. Side note: "Sexist, racist" is not at all the same as "Sexy, racy". How weird is that?]

After you let your dog back inside you plop yourself back at your desk and enjoy the final moments of the Windows 8 installer. It is glorious. The Windows 8 installer installs the shit out of Windows 8. Redmond should be proud. In fact, the installer is so excellent, a small tear develops in the corner of your eye -- and you are suddenly compelled to write a nice letter to Microsoft.

"Dear Microsoft Guys,

Thank you for the Windows 8 installer and how it installs the shit out of Windows 8.

Sincerely, NAME REDACTED"

As you finish spritzing your letter with just a dash of cologne (that's how Microsoft knows you care) the installer finishes it's epic task (that being to install Windows 8 which, as has been previously discussed, it does the shit out of). First things first: time to install a better web browser!

So you click on the old Internet Explorer icon -- taking a brief moment to marvel at how quickly it launched on your super duper new machine -- and... there's no Internet connection. Why is there no Internet connection?

Troubleshooting wizard? Huh? No. You can handle that

on your own.

Luckily, you're smarter than your average bear. You unplug the Ethernet cable from the back of your GENERIC BRAND VIDEO GAME CONSOLE and hook that up to your new PC tower. You know that connection works, you use it to play GAME ABOUT SHOOTING on the Internet with 12 year olds all the time.

Still no dice. And that little troubleshooting wizard is really starting to piss you off.

After much investigating (and swearing) you realize that Windows does not have the driver for your Ethernet card. So you'll need to go online to download it. Unfortunately you can't get online. Because you don't already have the driver that lets you get online. Which sort of makes you want to punch a hobo.

1) Go to library and use their Internet. - turn to part 9

2) Bag it. Try MacOS - turn to part 5

3) I bet Linux can access the Internet - turn to part 6

4) Who needs the Internet? Time for DOS! - turn to part 2

You get some frozen yogurt. It is incredible. Because it is frozen yogurt. And that's how the universe works.

1) Home. Windows. Install. - turn to part 7

Luckily you've got a USB flash drive ready. So you hop in the car and drive down to the library. It's only 3 blocks, but you're in a hurry here. No time for walking! You need Internet, man!

I'm not going to bore you with the tale of how you utilized one of the public library computers to search for, and download, the driver for the Ethernet card you have in your PC. Suffice to say: it happened as you would expect. Except for the whole "lifetime ban from ever setting foot in the library" thing. That feels a bit excessive. I mean, that guy was mostly bald already.

2 hours later, you return home, stick the flash drive in your tower and run the driver setup .exe.

At this point there is good news and bad news.

The Good News: You downloaded the wrong driver. Which means you still have no Internet.

The Bad News: You can't think of anyone nearby that you can beg to use their computer to download the right driver.

1) Head to the store and buy a new Ethernet card. - turn to part 10

2) There's always MacOS... - turn to part 5

3) Seriously. Internet. - turn to part 6

4) Who needs the Internet? Time for DOS! - turn to part 2

Feeling defeated -- and all alone in this cruel, cruel world -- you head back to the local Nerd Stuff to buy a new network card. This may seem like a drastic move to some, but you are a man with needs. Specifically, you need Internet access so that you can download and install updates to your new PC all night long.

"Welcome to Nerd Stuff! Anything I can help you find?" says the blue-shirted, happy man.

"I need a NIC."

"I'm sorry, what's that?"

You smile. But deep inside you want this man to die. "Ethernet card. I need an Ethernet card."

"Oh, no problem! Though you probably mean you want a wireless router"

You cut him off. "No. Ethernet card."

"Totally understand. Let me show you what we've got. Ah! Here's a great 802.11"

Again. Cut him off. Because he's an idiot. "No. Ethernet card."

"Hmm. I see. Hold one while I get someone from the computer department."

As the man heads off to find help, you finally allow yourself to breath and begin hunting for your new network card. Unfortunately there seems to be only one option. And it is the exact same card you already have. You are, needless to say, both bummed and frustrated.

Just then, inspiration strikes! You look around – like a super sneaky spy dude – to make sure nobody is looking. Then, acting as casually as possible, you pop open the box of the NIC.

Which is harder to open than you'd think, what with all that tape on the end. The box now looks like it was chewed on by a Tauntaun.

What's more... no CD inside. No driver. You just molested that poor box for nothing.

You casually place it back on the rack, angled so that the "chewed on" side is less visible, and try to decide what to do next.

1) Buy a copy of MacOS to install on your PC at home - turn to part 5

2) Just install Linux, already - turn to part 6

3) Hey, I heard DOS is pretty cool - turn to part 2

You get home, plop yourself down at your desk, turn on the PC and stick the MacOS install DVD in the drive.

And... it's... wait... something's not quite right...

About 20 reboots later you come to a pretty major decision: This isn't working. Apparently MacOS doesn't like something about your PC. Huh. You'd love to do some quick research to figure out what the problem is... but, you know... no working PC.

1) Back to the Apple Store for help! - turn to part 12

2) Give up and try Windows - turn to part 4

3) Why are you not using Linux? - turn to part 6

4) Desperate enough for DOS? - turn to part 2

You stroll into the Apple Store and head up to the first employee you see.

"Hey, I can't seem to get MacOS installed and I was hoping someone could," you get cut off before you can finish.

"Do you have an appointment?" asks the snarky little man.

"Well. No. I really just had a quick question about which components are compatible with," again you get cut off.

"You'll need an appointment for the Genius Bar."

...

You have no idea how to reply to what is, without a doubt, one of the single dumbest things you have ever heard. After, what seems like, several minutes of a stupidity-induced coma, you finally manage to reply. "Soooo..."

The man points to a big screen behind the "Genius Bar" – which, and this seems worth noting, looks just like a normal counter. "Is your name on that screen?"

It isn't. But, you have an idea.

"Hey, look over there!"

You hustle over to one of the "Geniuses" and the "Bar" and quickly explain your issue before the little turd figures out your clever ruse.

"You can't install Mac OS on a PC! Bwahahahaha! Hey everyone! This guy is trying to use MacOS on a boring old PC! Bwahahaha!" the genius laughs, the whole store joining in the gaiety.

1) Break down and buy a new Mac - turn to part 13

2) Just freaking install Windows - turn to part 4

3) L.I.N.U.X. - turn to part 6

Your will broken and, since you are already at the Apple Store, you decide to buy a Mac. Not an expensive Mac, mind you. Just something, anything, that you can actually use to, you know, do computery things with.

After selecting the cheapest Mac money can buy (which is still about twice as much as you built your PC for), and engaging in the full contact, mixed martial arts cage match that is required in order to decline Apple Care, you slowly head home. A defeated husk of a man.

Your next few days actually go pretty well. You get your shiny, new Mac setup easily enough and things seem to mostly be working without too much hassle.

As the weeks and months roll on you become convinced that your Mac is superior hardware to all other hardware – and that Mac OS is doubly superior to all other Operating Systems. This conviction quickly turns into an annoying habit where, every time a friend mentions a computer problem, you snarkily suggest getting a Mac.

You die alone. With your Mac. Because nobody likes you.

Game fucking over.

Part 14

Holy CRAP that is good froyo! You resolve to enjoy froyo more often. With sprinkles. Hell yes. Sprinkles like a mother fucker!

1) Get home and install Linux - turn to part 15

Computer on. Disc in. Boots right up. Even gives the option to test drive the system before installing it. How cool is that?

So you do the "test drive" just to be sure all of your hardware works – and it does – then you proceed to install to your hard drive. While the installer copies files around you decide to take advantage of the moment to take Scruffy for a walk.

While walking in the late afternoon sun, you reflect on what a great decision you made that day. Plus you saw a hot, nerdy college girl. Yessir, life is good.

By the time you return home your system is finished installing. A quick reboot later and you've got a fully working system.

Knock, knock, knock. What's that noise, you wonder? You resolve to check into it some day.

Knock, knock, knock. What the hell is... Oh. Right.

You open the front door to find... the college girl. She smiles at you. You blurt out something along the lines of "Hi I'm door". She holds up two tickets to Comic Con.

A man in a suit walks by on the sidewalk outside your home. He almost passes by, but then stops suddenly. "Hey! Did you just install Linux?"

"Uh-huh."

"Well, I'm looking for a new vice president to run my video game company. Interested?"

"Uh-huh."

"Great! You start tomorrow! But don't come to work before 10am. That's when the breakfast pizza is delivered."

"Okay."

The girl of your dreams turns to you. "Let's go to comic book and video game conventions together and have a very low-pressure relationship filled with lots and lots of uninhibited sex. Do you mind if I dress up like Princess Leia sometimes while we watch Star Wars in Machette Order?"

"Nope."

THE END

As time marches steadily onward, two things become face-punching-ly clear: I suck (rather spectacularly) at eating spaghetti without making a major damned mess... and Linux increases its level of Badassery at an exponential rate.

It is with this crucial truth in mind -- the Linux thing, not the spaghetti thing... I don't even know why I brought that up -- that I decided "Linux is Badass" deserved to be updated for 2014. If Linux is going to be so much more mind-exploding-ly amazing in 2014 than in 2013, so too must this book step up its game.

In the pages that follow you will gain a glimpse into my soul. That spark, deep down, that makes me who I am. That differentiates me from people who have normal jobs. My essence.

That's right. Poetry. About Linux. Often using the word "fuck".

"How does a bunch of dirty poetry explain how Linux is Badass? This book is shitty and Bryan Lunduke is an asshole."

An excellent question, random prick I just made up! I'll tell you!

If you can read a poem -- on any topic -- and, at the end, sit back and think to yourself, "that was pretty badass"... then that proves the topic of the poem itself to be of an extraordinary level of badassness. Case in point, that man from nantucket. (You know, the "There once was a man from Nantucket" guy.) That dude? Badass.

I also have a firm belief that most amazing things in this world can be ruthlessly ridiculed and, if they truly are as stellar as we think they are, they emerge looking even more badicall than before. Also, as that guy I made up a few paragraphs pointed out,

I'm an asshole. So many of these poems are making fun of Linux.

Because Linux is awesome. And it can take it.

Also the asshole thing.

"She took my dog, my truck and my gratuitous desktop effects."

Wobbly windows were so fucking tight.
I dream about them every damned night.

My windows popped out and looked all 3D.
It felt, a bit, like being on LSD.

And when I hit close, it all caught on fire.
It lifted my soul up higher and higher.

Oh, Compiz! Oh, Beryl! Where have these things gone?
Without them in my life, it's so hard to press on!

Don't fuck with me, man. I ain't no noob.
Just bring me back my damned spinning cube.

"Farewell, sweet XOrg"

Farewell, sweet X.Org, it's sure been swell.

And now we all wish you a fond farewell.

"Hey, I'm still here!", XOrg did yell.

I'm sorry to tell you, and I don't mean to dwell,

But Wayland is replacing you really quite well.

I understand that this may be a tough sell,

So here's a few bucks. Go find a motel.

"Woo! Debian Haiku Free-for-all!"

Debian is like
Ubuntu without all the
Stuff that pissed you off.

Debian is best
Summed up with three simple words:
It's not Fedora.

"Ubuntu Haiku Time"

Clean shaven space man!
Where's your crazy nerd neck beard?
Oh. Whoah. Too far, dude.

Convergence does not
Mean what I think you think it
means. Seriously.

"Linux Mint Haiku Party!"

This is Linux Mint
It is not just Ubuntu
Like, for serious

We are Linux Mint
License Ubuntu? No thanks
Living on the edge

"Why did I write this Haiku about Mageia?"

Isn't that Mandrake?

No? Really? Mandriva, then?

You messing with me?

"I blame Lennart Poettering with a classy haiku"

USB Sound Box.

Pulse Audio doesn't care.

No sound. Fuck my life.

"Limericks about package management"

There once was an old Yellow Dog.
That ran about as fast as a log.
So Seth made some YUM.
And boy, did it hum!
We threw that old YUP in a bog.

Why don't I ever use Aptitude?
It's like apt-get with so much more attitude.
There's "aptitude -v moo".
Which is pretty damned coo.
For Aptitude I should show more gratitude.

Zypper is so gosh darned reliable.
And its solver, so satisfiable.
Plus it's just fun to view.
When you type "zypper moo".
Its awesomeness is, indeed, verifiable.

I manage my system with Portage.
And, for source code, I need never forage.

I'll always be smiling.

While my software's compiling.

Just more time for me to... eat porridge.

"A treatise on the relative drawbacks and merits of Fedora"

Oh, Fedora! Why do you suck?

You keep saying that you don't suck.

But for reals. You suck.

Big donkey balls suck.

I mean damn. Come on. Holy fuck.

"MY EYES THEY BURN"

There once was good old Ubuntu

Who looked all orange and poo

I disliked it so much

And told them as such

They made it purple. Which also blew.

"Arch gets a limerick"

There once was a distro called Arch

With updates always on the march

I packman -Syu'd

And went out to get food

When I came back it was on a death march

Ok. That was a pretty lazy rhyme. Rhyming "march" with "march"? Lame. Plus, it doesn't really represent Arch that well. Perhaps that final line should read:

"When I came back my whole system was really fucked up and LibreOffice wouldn't fucking launch."

"Ode to Ubuntu's Unity Dash"

Oh, Ubuntu! Oh, Ubuntu!

Why are you so slow?

Oh, Ubuntu! Oh, Ubuntu!

Where's your get up and go?

I click on the Dash

And my hard drive just crunches.

So I click it again!

Oh, I hate it a bunches!

I click it some more!

I click it! I click it!

You're so friggin' pokey!

Why don't you do crossfit?

Oh, why don't you open?

I wait here for hours!

WHY DON'T YOU OPEN?!

I AM GOING TO FR…Oh, there it goes.

"The Complete History of Ubuntu (Abridged)"

Gather 'round, my friends and hear a most nerdy tale.
A tale about Linux (and a very small whale).

Our story begins back in nineteen ninety three.
With some dude named Ian, who had a girlfriend, you see.

Her name was Debra, if I'm remembering right.
So he put their names together, and made some Linux one night.

And so Debian was born from two names together.
(We're just lucky it wasn't "Brangelina" or "Bennifer".)

Fast forward, ye all, to two thousand and four.
When some astronaut dude wanted to make something more.

"This Debian's cool," he said. "I like it a lot!"
"But if it were orange and brown? Hot damn, that'd be hot!"

So he took his space money and started a team.
And created a warthog, the best we'd yet seen!

Oh, everyone loved it! Oh, everyone cheered!

Except those wearing red hats, or with a neck beard.

The spaceman got excited, "I know just what to do!"
"We'll build it for TVs and probably phones too!"

"There's no way we can lose! No way we can fail!"
Said the spaceman while riding a small, orange whale.